ALPHA
YOUTH
series

Alpha

DISCUSSION GUIDE

Alpha Youth Series Discussion Guide
© 2018 Alpha International

Requests for information should be addressed to:
HarperChristian Resources, 3900 Sparks Dr. SE, Grand Rapids, Michigan 49546

ISBN 978-0-310-09689-4

All Scripture quotations, unless otherwise indicated, are taken from *The Holy Bible, New International Version*®, NIV®. Copyright © 1973, 1978, 1984, 2011 by Biblica, Inc.® Used by permission of Zondervan. All rights reserved worldwide. www.Zondervan.com. The "NIV" and "New International Version" are trademarks registered in the United States Patent and Trademark Office by Biblica, Inc.®

Scripture quotations marked GNT taken from the Good News Translation, Second Edition, Copyright 1992 by American Bible Society. Used by Permission.

Scripture quotations marked NLT are taken from are taken from the Holy Bible, New Living Translation, copyright © 1996, 2004, 2007 by Tyndale House Foundation. Used by permission of Tyndale House Publishers, Inc., Carol Stream, Illinois 60188. All rights reserved.

Scripture quotations marked Phillips taken from The New Testament in Modern English, Revised Edition, J. B. Phillips, Translator. © J. B. Phillips 1958, 1960, 1972. Used by permission of Macmillan Publishing Co., Inc., 866 Third Avenue, New York, NY 10022.

The Alpha name and trademarks are used under license from Alpha International.
Alpha USA, PO Box 7491, Carol Stream, IL 60197-7491

All rights reserved. No portion of this publication may be reproduced, stored in a retrieval system, or transmitted in any form or by any means—electronic, mechanical, photocopy, recording, scanning, or other—without the prior written consent of the publisher. Where an Alpha publication is offered free of charge, the fee is waived on condition the publication is used to run or promote Alpha and should not be subject to any subsequent fee or charge. This resource may not be modified or used for any commercial purpose without permission in writing from the copyright holder or the expressly authorized agent thereof.

Any internet addresses (websites, blogs, etc.) and telephone numbers in this study guide are offered as a resource. They are not intended in any way to be or imply an endorsement by HarperChristian Resources, nor does HarperChristian Resources vouch for the content of these sites and numbers for the life of this study guide.

HarperChristian Resources titles may be purchased in bulk for church, business, fundraising, or ministry use. For information, please e-mail ResourceSpecialist@ChurchSource.com.

First Printing August 2018 / *Printed in the United States of America*

INTRODUCTION

A note from Jason and Ben
(Hosts of the Alpha Youth Series)

Dear Small Group Host,

Here's the secret about Alpha: small groups are the most important part.

We spent thousands of hours making the Alpha Youth Series,
but it's just a spark. The impact is because of people like you; small
group hosts who take the spark and lead a conversation where
people feel heard, respected, and loved. That's what people will
remember and that's what will impact their lives. **We need *you* more
than you need the videos.**

We are praying for you as you encounter bizarre questions, awkward
silences and stunning stories. You are going to do a great job. Keep
one ear to the guests and the other to Jesus. It's not the words that
you share, but the way you listen, that will make the difference.

With love in Jesus,

**Jason Ballard and Ben Woodman
and the whole team at Alpha**

HOW TO USE

This Discussion Guide is a tool that can help every Alpha small group host. Each chapter corresponds to an episode.

It highlights the important points, helps you remember the key quotes and Bible verses, and provides you with loads of intriguing discussion questions to keep things lively. Use it to get an idea of where the episode is going and what's been covered. It's designed to help you, not limit you. It's all here as a springboard to help you take the conversation further than you could without it.

Not a secret

Don't feel like you need to keep the content of this guide a secret from the guests at your table. We wrote it knowing that someone in your small group will want to steal it from you to see what's in here. Guests will be excited to know that you have some of the quotes and verses handy so you can come back to them in conversation.

Three questions

Each episode is designed to be **paused three times** for group discussion (prompted by on-screen questions and street interviews). A countdown signals the end of each discussion break. The street interviews are meant to spark ideas and opinions and help create conversation. We've highlighted these questions in the discussion guide so you know what's coming and where you are in the session.

Supporting questions

Sometimes the question on the screen doesn't spark enough conversation so we have included several supporting questions to help you keep the chat alive and capture the imagination of guests. Don't feel limited to these. You can be creative and throw some other questions into the mix.

More questions

The three breaks for conversation throughout each episode are just the beginning. We have included a handful of follow-up questions to help you lead a time of discussion after each episode is done. We recommend 10–20 minutes. Don't feel like you need to follow these questions exactly. Choose a few, mix up the order, and add your own. Let the conversation grow naturally as the guests respond with their own questions from the episode.

Register online

If you haven't already, register your Alpha online. In the USA, register at run.alphausa.org; in Canada, register at run.alphacanada.org. By registering, you will be given **free access to a suite of support materials** to help you plan, promote, and run Alpha.

Features:
- Digital Discussion Guide
- Customizable promotional materials
- Sample session schedules
- Trailers

TIPS AND GUIDELINES
FOR HOSTING DISCUSSION

Discussion in small groups is the most important part of every Alpha session. Hosting a discussion on Alpha is not about re-teaching any of the content from the episode – the goal is to create a safe place where everyone can share openly and honestly about their thoughts and feelings and ask questions. Remember, the Discussion Guide is just a guide. Use these questions to initiate conversation and bring it back on track when needed.

Alpha is a journey. The more time you spend together as a group, the more people will feel free to open up and share their opinions.

Tips for hosts and helpers

- Remember names
- Pray
- Be committed
- Show up early to welcome guests
- Stay long enough to chat with guests afterwards
- Keep the conversation alive and balanced
- Be encouraging
- End on time
- If time allows, debrief with your Alpha team to celebrate wins, chat about challenges and share prayer requests

Guidelines for the group

Read this at least once to your group and maybe a second or third time during Alpha as a reminder.

- You don't have to talk if you don't want to
- You can ask or say just about anything (as long as you aren't putting other people down or preventing others from talking)
- Respect each other by listening and allowing different opinions
- Keep things confidential when you leave the group

Be sure to watch our three training episodes to get everything you need to be the best possible host and helper.

LIFE: IS THIS IT?

Big idea

Alpha is an invitation to explore life's biggest questions and a chance to look at the life and message of Jesus. Every opinion and question is welcome.

Remind yourself of the tips and guidelines for hosting discussion on page 7, and remember to share the guidelines for the group:

- You don't have to talk if you don't want to
- You can ask or say just about anything (as long as you aren't putting other people down or preventing others from talking)
- Respect each other by listening and allowing different opinions
- Keep things confidential when you leave the group

Q1
If you had 24 hours to do anything, what would you do?

Imagine money is limitless and travel is instant.

If you haven't already, give everyone a chance to introduce themselves. Keep it light. There will be time to get to the deeper stuff later.

Supporting questions
- What's something you have always wanted to do? (Bucket list.)
- Where have you always wanted to travel?

Q2
What makes you happy?

Supporting questions
- What could you not live without?
- Have you ever had too much of a good thing?

Q3
If it turned out God existed after all, and you could ask one question, what would it be?

As people answer this question, write down the answers so you can look back at them in later weeks.

Supporting questions
- Where do people go to talk about these sorts of questions?
- Why do people sometimes find it awkward to talk about big life and faith questions?

More questions

Many groups leave 10–20 minutes after the episode is done for more conversation.

- How did you end up at Alpha?
- What did you think/feel about this episode?
- What stood out to you from this episode?
- Do you have any hopes or expectations about doing Alpha?

In each one of our hearts, it's like we have a happiness bucket that we're constantly trying to fill.

"I am the bread of life."
Jesus, John 6:35

"Christianity, if false, is of no importance, and if true, of infinite importance. The only thing it cannot be is moderately important."
C.S. Lewis

"I am the way and the truth and the life."
Jesus, John 14:6

JESUS: WHO IS HE?

Big idea

Jesus Christ is the most famous person in history and there's evidence to suggest Jesus was more than a great religious teacher. His life, death and resurrection is the centerpiece of the Christian faith. The resurrection not only suggests that God exists, but also that God has revealed himself through Jesus.

Remind yourself of the tips and guidelines for hosting discussion on page 7, and it may be helpful to share the guidelines for the group again:

- You don't have to talk if you don't want to
- You can ask or say just about anything (as long as you aren't putting other people down or preventing others from talking)
- Respect each other by listening and allowing different opinions
- Keep things confidential when you leave the group

Q1
What would you want to be famous for?

If you haven't already, give everyone a chance to introduce themselves again.

Supporting questions
- Have you ever had an encounter with a celebrity?
- If you could meet any celebrity, who would it be? Why?

Q2
Why do you think Jesus is so famous?

Supporting questions
- What is Jesus most known for?
- What stands out most to you about Jesus?

Q3
Who do people think Jesus is?

Supporting questions
- Why do you think there are so many different opinions about Jesus?
- What do you think about the things Jesus said and taught?
  (*"I am the way," "love your enemies," " am the life," "I am the truth,"
  "I am the bread of life," "I and the Father are one."*)

More questions

Many groups leave 10–20 minutes after the episode is done for more conversation.

- Did anything from the episode stand out to you?
- What do you think it would have been like to be around Jesus?
- What parts of the life of Jesus stand out to you?
- (Examples from the episode: his teaching, his claims, healing, his death on a cross, his resurrection from the dead, his compassion for the outcasts.)
- Why do you think Jesus spent so much time with outcasts, the sick and the poor?
- What do you think about the claim that Jesus is God?

When other religious teachers might say, "This is the way to full life," Jesus said, "I am the life." When others might say, "Here is the truth", Jesus said, "I am the truth."

"Come to me, all you who are weary and burdened, and I will give you rest."
Jesus, Matthew 11:28

"Christianity is not an emotion – it's not true because I want it to be true. It's true because the actual tomb is empty. It's based on a historical event."
Mark Clark

"I and the Father are one."
Jesus, John 10:3

CROSS: WHY DID JESUS DIE?

Big idea

This session is all about the question, why did Jesus die? Although sin has real consequences, Jesus' death and resurrection are the solution to the problem of sin. The cross shows us that God loves us, death has been defeated, the power of sin has been broken and we can have a relationship with our heavenly Father.

Remind yourself of the tips and guidelines for hosting discussion on page 7. It may be helpful to share the guidelines for the group again, particularly if you have any new members:

Guidelines for the group

- You don't have to talk if you don't want to
- You can ask or say just about anything (as long as you aren't putting other people down or preventing others from talking)
- Respect each other by listening and allowing different opinions
- Keep things confidential when you leave the group

Q1
What is the best (or worst) thing you've ever made?

If you haven't already, give everyone a chance to introduce themselves again.

Supporting questions
- What's the best or worst thing you've ever cooked/baked?
- Have you ever made something in school that you (or your parents) have kept?

Q2
How do you see sin in the world around you?

Supporting questions
- Where do you see evil in your school, your city, your country, and the world?
- How has sin affected you personally?

Q3
What does forgiveness mean to you?

Supporting questions
- Think about a time you had to forgive someone. Why did you do it?
- Why do you think the message of forgiveness is so central to Christianity?

More questions

Many groups leave 10–20 minutes after the episode is done for more conversation.

- Did anything from the episode stand out for you?
- What comes to mind when you think about the cross?
- When the hosts talked about the four consequences of sin (partition, penalty, power, pollution), which stood out most to you? Why?
- What do you think about the claim that Jesus is the solution to our problem of sin?
- How did you feel about the scene at the end with the father and the son?

"The Son of God... loved me and gave himself for me."
Galatians 2:20

"...all have sinned and fall short of the glory of God."
Romans 3:23

Jesus' death and resurrection are God's solution to the problem of sin.

"...the LORD has laid on him (on Jesus) the iniquity of us all."
Isaiah 53:6

God loves you, Jesus died for you, and through the cross, we are invited into a relationship with God.

FAITH: HOW CAN I HAVE FAITH?

Make sure to mention the details of your upcoming Alpha Weekend.
Let your group know where, when, and what it is.

Big idea

The big question this episode explores is, what does it mean to be a Christian? Or, in other words, what does it mean to have faith? Christianity is not a club someone joins or a set of ideas to add to your knowledge. It is a life-changing relationship with Jesus! And we enter into that relationship by faith – not blind faith, but a step of faith based on the truth about who Jesus is and what he has done.

Q1
What kind of club would you start or join?

Supporting questions
- When you're retired what do you think your hobbies will be?
- What hobbies have you had over the years?

Q2
What do you think about Christianity being described in terms of a relationship with God?

Supporting questions
- What are some qualities or characteristics of a good relationship?
- How would a relationship with God be different from a relationship with someone else?

Q3

If this pool represents a relationship with God, which character do you most identify with?

Show the group the picture of the characters at the pool from page 19.

Supporting questions

- What is it about that character that stands out to you the most?
- If you've seen this picture before, has your choice of character changed from last time?
- If you could add another character to represent yourself, what would it be like?

More questions

Many groups leave 10–20 minutes after the episode is done for more conversation.

- What stood out to you from this episode?
- Jason said, "The one who knows you the best, is the one who loves you the most." What do you think about that statement? Or how do you feel about it?
- What are some obstacles that might prevent you from having a relationship with God?
- After four weeks of Alpha what are the big questions on your mind? What are you hoping might come up in future weeks?
- What does the idea "a step of faith" mean to you? What does that have to do with Christianity?

"This means that anyone who belongs to Christ has become a new person. The old life is gone; a new life has begun!"
2 Corinthians 5:17

"Here I am! I stand at the door and knock. If anyone hears my voice and opens the door, I will come in and eat with that person, and they with me."
Revelation 3:20

A great description of the word "faith" is trusting someone (or something) enough to act on that trust.

"To all who believed him (Jesus) and accepted him, he gave the right to become children of God."
John 1:12

PRAYER: WHY AND HOW DO I PRAY?

This episode ends with a short prayer. At the end of the discussion time, try praying together with your small group. You might simply say a short prayer or give guests an opportunity to pray out loud. In the following weeks, hosts can choose to end discussion time with prayer.

Big idea

Simply put, prayer is talking with God. Jesus makes it possible for us to have a personal relationship with God. Just like all of our relationships, our relationship with God grows through communication. Through prayer, God transforms situations, gives us peace, changes our perspective and shows us more of what he is like.

Q1
If you could have a superpower, what would it be?

Supporting questions
- What is the worst superpower?
- Who is your favorite superhero?

Q2
Why do you think people don't always get what they pray for?

Supporting questions
- What questions come to mind when you think about prayer?
- If you were in charge of answering prayers, how would you decide how to respond?

Q3

**Have you ever tried praying?
How did it go?**

Supporting questions

- If you had to describe prayer to someone, what would you say?
- How do you feel about the idea that God is with us when we are struggling?

More questions

*Many groups leave 10–20 minutes after the episode is done for more
conversation.*

- What do you think about this episode?
- Did any specific moments or stories stand out to you?
- If God knows all of our needs, why does the Bible tell us to pray?
- Ben talked about going through a challenging time and experiencing
  peace when he prayed. Have you ever experienced anything like that?
- What do you think about the tips on prayer that Landry and Jassie gave?
  Keep it real, keep it simple, keep it going.

Key quotes and scriptures

"But when you pray, go into your room, close the
door and pray to your Father, who is unseen. Then your
Father, who sees what is done in secret will reward you."
Matthew 6:6

You can pray about anything - little things and big things. God cares about everything, from what's happening in your family, to what's happening around the world.

"Do not be anxious about anything, but in every situation, by prayer and petition, with thanksgiving, present your requests to God. And the peace of God, which transcends all understanding, will guard your hearts and your minds in Christ Jesus."
Philippians 4:6-7

"When a train goes through a tunnel and it gets dark, you don't throw away the ticket and jump off. You sit still and trust the driver."
Corrie ten Boom

"For through him (Jesus) we both have access to the Father by one Spirit."
Ephesians 2:18

BIBLE: WHY AND HOW DO I READ THE BIBLE?

Make sure to mention the details of your upcoming Alpha Weekend.
Remind your group where, when, and what it is.

Big idea

> The Bible is the primary way God speaks to us and reveals himself to us. The Bible points us to Jesus and gives us instructions for living. Through the Bible, we're invited to connect with God and build a day-to-day relationship with Jesus.

Q1
Imagine you are being stranded on a deserted island and you can only bring three things with you. What would they be?

Supporting questions
- If your house was burning down, and all your family and pets and phone were totally safe, what one thing would you take with you?
- What is your favorite book? (If someone says "the Bible", ask for their second favorite book.)

Q2
What do you think the purpose of the Bible is today?

Supporting questions
- Do you think the ideas in the Bible are old-fashioned or outdated?
- Do you think the Bible is worth reading today? Why or why not?

Q3

Have you ever tried reading the Bible?
How did it go?

Supporting questions

Do any quotes from the Bible stand out or have special meaning to you?
Have you ever heard somebody teach from the Bible and connected with it?

More questions

Many groups leave 10–20 minutes after the episode is done for more conversation.

- What do you think about today's episode?
- Did anything stand out to you?
- What are your biggest questions when it comes to the Bible?
- How do you feel about the idea of God speaking to us through the Bible?
- Jassie and Peter gave seven tips for reading the Bible (get a Bible, find a time and place, don't flip and point, genre matters, ask lots of questions, pray, talk to people). Which of these, if any, stands out to you?
- Why would governments not want the Bible in their country?

The Bible is a guide – it shows us how to live and it gives us boundaries.

God's word is our highest authority for what we believe and for how we live.

"All scripture is inspired by God and is useful to teach us what is true and to make us realise what is wrong in our lives. It corrects us when we are wrong and teaches us to do what is right. God uses it to prepare and equip his people to do every good work."
2 Timothy 3:16–17

"Reading the Bible generates life. It produces change.
It heals hurts. It builds character. It transforms circumstances.
It imparts joy. It overcomes adversity. It defeats temptation.
It infuses hope. It releases power. It cleanses the mind."
Rick Warren

SPIRIT: WHO IS THE HOLY SPIRIT AND WHAT DOES HE DO?

Big idea

The Holy Spirit is God with us. He is God with you! He is a source of strength and freedom. He brings change in our character. The Spirit gives us power to serve, and he fills our hearts with the love of God.

Q1
What do you find scary?

Supporting questions
- What's the strangest phobia that you've ever heard of?
- As a kid, what was your biggest fear?

Q2
What comes to mind when you think about the Holy Spirit?

Supporting questions
- The Bible uses many names when referring to the Holy Spirit. Do any of them stand out to you? (Comforter, Advocate, Spirit of Wisdom, Guide, Teacher, Gift of God, Spirit of Jesus, and Helper.)
- Do any questions come to mind when you hear about the activity of the Holy Spirit through history?

Q3

If you could have more of any of these, which one would most impact your life today? Love, joy, peace, patience, kindness, goodness, faithfulness, gentleness and self-control.

Supporting questions

- What do you think about the idea that the Holy Spirit produces more love, joy and peace in our lives?
- What do you think about the idea that the Holy Spirit brings freedom to our lives?
- What do you think about the Holy Spirit giving us courage to tell others about Jesus?

More Questions

Many groups leave 10–20 minutes after the episode is done for more conversation.

- What do you think about today's episode?
- What stood out to you most in today's episode?
- How do you feel about the idea that God is present with us through his Holy Spirit?
- Have you ever had someone pray with you? How did it go?
- Open up the Bible to 1 Corinthians 12:4–11, read the text and then lead a short conversation about it.
  - Have you ever heard of or had any experience with God's supernatural gifts?
  - What questions come to mind when you hear this passage?

"I will give you a new heart and put a new spirit in you; I will remove from you your heart of stone and give you a heart of flesh. And I will put my Spirit in you..."
Ezekiel 36:26

"The Holy Spirit produces this kind of fruit in our lives: love, joy, peace, patience, kindness, goodness, faithfulness, gentleness, and self-control."
Galatians 5:22–23

The Holy Spirit isn't some vague supernatural force.
He's a person.

The Holy Spirit was present at the creation of the universe.
He breathed life into the very first people.

"You will receive power when the Holy Spirit comes on you; and you will be my witnesses in Jerusalem, and in all Judea and Samaria, and to the ends of the earth."
Jesus, Acts 1:8

"God says, 'In the last days, I will pour out my Spirit upon all people. Your sons and daughters will prophesy. Your old men will dream dreams, and your young men will see visions. In those days I will pour out my Spirit even on servants – men and women alike'."
Joel 2:28-29

"The Spirit of the Lord is on me, because he has anointed me to proclaim good news to the poor. He has sent me to proclaim freedom for the prisoners and recovery of sight for the blind, to set the oppressed free, to proclaim the year of the Lord's favor."
Jesus, Luke 4:18-19

"The Holy Spirit produces this kind of fruit in our lives: love, joy, peace, patience, kindness, goodness, faithfulness, gentleness, and self-control."
Galatians 5:22-23

FILL: HOW CAN I BE FILLED WITH THE HOLY SPIRIT?

There are no discussion questions during this episode and no discussion questions afterwards. This episode is meant to serve as preparation for a time of prayer.

To prepare for this session, be sure to watch the Team Training session on ***Prayer Ministry and the Alpha Weekend****.*

Big idea

God wants all of us to experience being filled with his Holy Spirit. When the Holy Spirit fills our lives, our experience is marked by a profound sense of God's love and power, boldness to tell others, and a renewed desire to praise God. This experience is unique for each person.

Guidelines for this session

For many, this prayer time is the most impactful part of Alpha. Set aside 15-45 minutes for prayer and songs of worship following the episode. The goal is to make space for God and to give everyone the opportunity to receive prayer if they would like.

NEW LIFE: HOW CAN I MAKE THE MOST OF THE REST OF MY LIFE?

Big idea

A relationship with God changes everything. Because of God's great love for us, we can live a new life! No matter what kind of past you have had, God invites us to make the most of the rest of our lives. The new life that God invites us into is a life lived in response to his love.

Q1
If you could go back in time and give your past self some advice, what would you say?

Supporting questions
- What do you think the younger version of yourself would think about you today?

Q2
How have you felt pressured to fit in?

Supporting questions
- This session talks about the way of Jesus being different from the ways of this world. What do you think about that idea?
- Have you ever noticed yourself making a decision to do something just because the people around you were doing it?

Q3

How do you feel about the idea that God has a purpose for your life?

Supporting questions

- Do you think a relationship with God should impact our actions and the way we live?
- Do you find it hard to trust God (or someone else) with your future? Why or why not?

More questions

Many groups leave 10–20 minutes after the episode is done for more conversation.

- How did you feel about this episode?
- Did anything from the episode stand out to you?
- What do you think about the idea of "making the most of your life"?
- How do you feel about the idea of having a "fresh start" in life?
- In the previous session, how was your experience during the time of prayer around being filled with God's Spirit?
  If appropriate you may wish to offer an opportunity for the group to pray for each other.

Key quotes and scriptures

"If only we could live two lives: the first in which to make one's mistakes, and the second in which to profit by them."
D.H. Lawrence

"... anyone who belongs to Christ has become a new person. The old life is gone; a new life has begun!"
2 Corinthians 5:17

"Don't let the world around you squeeze you into its mold."
Romans 12:2

"But seek first his kingdom and his righteousness, and all these things will be given to you as well."
Jesus, Matthew 6:33

"Therefore, I urge you, brothers and sisters, in view of God's mercy, (in view of everything God has done for you) to offer your bodies as a living sacrifice, (in other words, offer every part of your life) holy and pleasing to God – this is your true and proper worship. Do not conform to the pattern of this world, but be transformed by the renewing of your mind. Then you will be able to test and approve what God's will is – his good, pleasing and perfect will."
Romans 12:1-2

EVIL: HOW CAN I RESIST EVIL?

Big idea

There are three forces of evil: the world (evil around us); the flesh (evil within us); the devil (spiritual forces of evil). The devil hates God and wants to destroy what's closest to God's heart – us! Three of his primary tactics are temptation, accusation and lies. We can stand firm against the devil's attacks and more than that, with God we can overcome evil with good!

Q1

If you had the power to solve one of the world's big problems, which problem would you solve? Why?

Supporting questions

- If you had the power to solve one of your school's (or city's) big problems, which would you solve? Why?
- Where do you think you can make the biggest difference in the world?

Q2

What are some common lies we believe about ourselves? About God?

Supporting questions

- Do you think that people have misconceptions about God? What are some of these?
- Every one of us wrestles with ideas about ourselves (for example, that we aren't loved, we aren't good enough, or we're not accepted). How can we learn to identify these ideas as lies and not let them have power in our lives?

Q3

What can people do to fight against evil in the world?

Supporting questions

- How can a group like ours make a positive difference in our communities?
- Who is someone you look up to who is impacting the world in positive ways?

More questions

Many groups leave 10–20 minutes after the episode is done for more conversation.

- What did you think about the episode?
- Did anything from the episode stand out to you?
- How is/was your experience on the Alpha Weekend? Did any moment stand out to you?
- Where do you think temptation comes from?
- How do you resist temptation?
- When you give in to temptation, how does it feel?
- How would you describe the devil's tactic of accusation? What are some examples of that?
- What do you think about the idea of "overcoming evil with good"?
- Did anything stand out to you from Peter and Jassie's description of the armor of God?

"The thief comes only to steal and kill and destroy; I have come that they may have life, and have it to the full."
Jesus, John 10:10

"Darkness cannot drive out darkness; only light can do that. Hate cannot drive out hate; only love can do that."
Martin Luther King Jr.

"Now there is no condemnation for those who belong to Christ Jesus."
Romans 8:1

"Some believe it is only great power that can hold evil in check, but that is not what I have found. It is the small everyday deeds of ordinary folk that keep the darkness at bay. Small acts of kindness and love."
J.R.R. Tolkien

"Resist the devil, and he will flee from you. Draw near to God, and he will draw near to you."
James 4:7-8

Your life can make a real difference.

"(God) has rescued us from the dominion of darkness and brought us into the kingdom of the Son he loves."
Colossians 1:13

"Do not be overcome by evil, but overcome evil with good."
Romans 12:21

"Finally, be strong in the Lord and in his mighty power. Put on the full armor of God, so that you can take your stand against the devil's schemes. For our struggle is not against flesh and blood, but against the rulers, against the authorities, against the powers of this dark world and against the spiritual forces of evil in the heavenly realms. Therefore put on the full armour of God, so that when the day of evil comes, you may be able to stand your ground, and after you have done everything, to stand."
Ephesians 6:10-13

TELLING OTHERS: WHY AND HOW SHOULD I TELL OTHERS?

Big idea

The message about Jesus is the best news anyone could ever hear! Because of who Jesus is and what he has done, we can have a relationship with God! With gentleness and respect, we can tell others about our faith and experience. Our words, prayers and loving actions all make a difference.

Q1
What is your most embarrassing moment?

Supporting questions
- What is the most embarrassing thing you have ever witnessed?

Q2
Is it okay to talk about our personal faith with others? Why or why not?

Supporting questions
- Is there a "right" or "wrong" time to talk about faith with people?
- Why can it be so awkward to talk about things like faith, spirituality and religion?

Q3
What should the impact of Christians be in society?

Supporting questions
- This session talks about how sharing the gospel is done through both words and loving actions.
  - What does that mean to you?
  - Where have you seen this? Or not seen this?

More questions

Many groups leave 10–20 minutes after the episode is done for more conversation.

- What do you think about today's episode?
- Did anything from the episode stand out to you?
- How was your experience on the Alpha Weekend? Did any moment stand out to you?
- There was a cartoon about how Ben's dad heard about Jesus while hitchhiking.
  - What do you think about that story?
  - How do you think the driver felt after he dropped them off?
- Danielle Strickland told a story about a boy sharing lunch with a friend at school.
  - What kind of needs or opportunities like that do you see around you?
- What do you think about the idea of you and a few friends running Alpha for some of your other friends?
- What would you say to someone who is afraid or nervous to talk to other people about their faith?

"You are the salt of the earth... You are the light of the world... let your light shine before others, so that they may see your good works and give glory to your Father who is in heaven."
Jesus, Matthew 5:13,14,16

"Always be prepared to give an answer to everyone who asks you to give the reason for the hope that you have. But do this with gentleness and respect."
1 Peter 3:15

A relationship with Jesus brings peace and joy. God fills our hearts with love. He brings meaning and purpose to our lives. He forgives us and offers us eternal life.

"All I know is that I once was blind and now I see."
John 9:25

"Our gospel came to you not simply with words but also with power, with the Holy Spirit and with deep conviction."
1 Thessalonians 1:5

HEALING: DOES GOD HEAL TODAY?

Big idea

God invites us to play a part in bringing healing to others.
The Gospels are full of stories of how Jesus healed people
miraculously. What we see in the New Testament and throughout
history is that God uses his followers to do the same. While we
may not fully understand why God heals some people and not
others, we keep asking because we can trust that he is a good
and loving Father.

Q1
What technology would you love to see invented?

Supporting questions
- What do you think is the worst ever invention?
- Other than your phone, laptop, tv, or tablet, what piece of technology do
  you use the most?

Q2
What do you think about the idea that God heals
people today?

Supporting questions
- What kind of questions come to mind when you think about God healing
  people?
- How do you see the relationship between medical intervention and
  miraculous healing?

Q3

Take a few minutes to talk about any experiences you've had praying for healing. Share any stories you've heard of God healing someone.

Supporting questions

- Physical healing isn't the only type of healing someone can experience. What are some other ways someone could be healed?
- Did any of the stories from this episode stand out to you?
- How do we make sense of the times God doesn't heal someone when we ask?

More questions

For this session, instead of taking more time for discussion, take 10–15 minutes to pray for each other for healing.

- You can take a few minutes to talk about questions that people might have after the episode.
- Explain that you are going to take some time to pray for each other and that no one has to pray or receive prayer if they don't want to.
- Ask if anyone has specific prayer requests for healing. They don't have to be specific if they don't want to.
- If one of the leaders shared words of knowledge about what God might want to heal, you can ask if anyone in your group connects with what was shared.
- Ask if one or two from the group would like to pray for the person who needs healing.
- This is also an opportunity to pray for people to be filled with the Holy Spirit and to pray for any other issues that are brought up.

"I am the Lord, who heals you."
Exodus 15:26

"Jesus went through all the towns and villages, teaching in their synagogues, proclaiming the good news of the kingdom and healing every disease and sickness."
Matthew 9:35

When Jesus heals people, it is like a taste of the future. It tells us that one day everyone is going to be healed.

"We're free and able to ask the Holy Spirit at any time to heal us. But if the Spirit does not do it, there's no reason to think that it's because we have no faith, or that God does not love us, or that God is punishing us."
Father Raniero Cantalamessa

CHURCH: WHAT ABOUT THE CHURCH?

Big idea

The church is the family of God. It's people, not a building. It's a movement of hope, love and justice. We are all invited to live out our faith in community with other believers. God works through the church to extend love to the whole world.

Q1

How have you enjoyed Alpha so far? Any highlights?

Supporting questions
- What has stood out to you most about your experience of Alpha so far?
- Did anything surprise you about your experience of Alpha?

Q2

What has your experience been with the church?

Supporting questions
- When you think about the church, what questions come to mind?
- What are some misunderstandings people have about the church?
- What do you think about the idea that "church is a people, not a building"?

Q3

If this pool represents a relationship with God, which character do you identify with the most?

Show pool picture (page 19).

Supporting questions

- Has your answer to this question changed from the beginning of your time on Alpha?
- Is there a missing character? Which other person might you add to describe where you are at?
- What do you think it would look like for you to take a step into the pool? Is anything holding you back?

More questions

Many groups leave 10–20 minutes after the episode is done for more conversation.

- How do you feel about this episode? Did anything from the episode stand out to you?
- In this session, five pictures represented the church: friends, family, home, body of Jesus, and love.
    - Do any of those images stand out to you?
    - Is there an idea or image that raised some questions for you?
- The church is so diverse in its expression. How can such a global and diverse church be united?
- Now that Alpha is coming to an end, how would you summarise your experience?
- Is there anyone in your life who you would want to invite to Alpha in the future?
- Looking forward, how can you continue the conversation and the journey you've started on Alpha?
- End your final small group time in prayer.

"There is a lot of unrest in the world and people are searching to find a place of family and home."
Laura Toganivalu

"When you love Jesus, you love those whom he loves."
Cardinal Tagle

When the church is operating as Jesus intended, it's a force for profound hope and healing in the world.

"Let us not neglect our meeting together, as some people do, but encourage one another..."
Hebrews 10:25

"For where two or three gather in my name, there am I with them."
Jesus, Matthew 18:20

"Now you are the body of Christ, and each one of you is a part of it."
1 Corinthians 12:27

"What unites us is infinitely greater than what divides us."
Nicky Gumbel

In John 17:21, Jesus prayed "that we may be one" – united – "so that the world will believe".

"We are being built together to become a dwelling in which God lives by his Spirit."
Ephesians 2:22

Alpha is just the beginning. Your journey has just begun. Following Jesus is life's great adventure!